The Caribbean Sea

By **Leighton Taylor**

Featuring the photographs of

Norbert Wu

BLACKBIRCH PRESS, INC.

WOODBRIDGE, CONNECTICUT

Published by Blackbirch Press, Inc.
260 Amity Road
Woodbridge, CT 06525

©1999 by Blackbirch Press, Inc.
First Edition

e-mail: staff@blackbirch.com
Web site: www.blackbirch.com

All photographs ©Norbert Wu/Mo Yung Productions, except: p. 3: PhotoDisc; p. 23: ©Mark Conlin/ Mo Yung Productions; p. 8: Courtesy NASA

Text ©Leighton Taylor

Printed in the United States

10 9 8 7 6 5 4 3 2 1

Editor's Note
The photos that appear on pages 23 and 37, show species that are found in the Caribbean Sea, but the photos were taken in a different locale. Because no suitable images of the species could be found in a Caribbean Sea environment, these very similar images were used instead.

Library of Congress Cataloging-in-Publication Data
Taylor, L.R. (Leighton R.)
The Caribbean sea / by Leighton Taylor ; featuring the photographs of Norbert Wu
    p.   cm. — (Life in the sea)
   Summary: In text and photographs, presents information about the Caribbean Sea, its location, physical environment, animal life, islands, and mysteries.
   ISBN 1-56711-244-7 (alk. paper)
   1. Caribbean Sea—Juvenile literature. [1. Caribbean Sea.]
I. Wu, Norbert. II. Title. III. Series: Taylor, L.R. (Leighton R.) Life in the sea.
GC531.T39   1999
551.46'35—dc21   98-9875
                                                               CIP
                                                               AC

IMAGINE A CRYSTAL BLUE SEA

Imagine a crystal blue sea where warm winds blow gently across the waves. Under the waves, thousands of species of brightly colored animals swim and crawl about, searching their surroundings for food, trying not to become food themselves. Imagine water filled with shells and fishes of neon and day-glow, some so bright it is hard to believe they are real.

ut you don't have to imagine! The Caribbean Sea is such a place! It is the most "American" of all the seas in the world. On one side of it is the Gulf of Mexico. Oceanographers call the Caribbean Sea and the Gulf of Mexico the "Central American Sea." The Gulf of Mexico touches the shores of southern U.S. states, such as Texas and Florida, and parts of Mexico. Water flows into the Gulf of Mexico from the Caribbean Sea but they are two separate parts of the Central American Sea.

Palms sway along the sandy shores of the Caribbean island of St. Kitts.

The Caribbean is home to many bright creatures, including this fairy basslet.

The Caribbean touches the very tip of Florida and its small islands. It also washes the shores of Mexico and many other countries. These include the Central American countries of Belize, Guatemala, Nicaragua, Costa Rica, Panama, and the South American countries of Colombia and Venezuela.

The Caribbean Sea is filled with many islands that belong to many countries. Cuba, Haiti, Dominican Republic, Jamaica, the Bahamas, and the Cayman Islands are just a few of the countries on Caribbean islands. France, England, and the Netherlands also have control of some Caribbean islands.

A THIN WALL OF LAND

Only a slender stretch of land separates the Caribbean Sea from the Pacific Ocean. Millions of years ago, there was no land separating the Pacific and the Caribbean. Fish could swim between the sea and the ocean.

Then, earthquakes and volcanoes pushed the sea bottom up above sea level. This new land connected the continents of North and South America. For land animals, this new land was a bridge; for sea animals, it was a wall. Land animals such as ancient camels, horses, and opossums could move from one continent to the other. But the land separated the Pacific Ocean from the Caribbean Sea. Fish could no longer swim between the sea and the ocean. Almost a hundred years ago, people dug a big canal called the Panama Canal across this thin wall of land so ships could go back and forth.

Because they once shared the same waters, the fish, crabs, corals, sponges, and other ocean animals in the Pacific and the Caribbean are closely related and look similar. But they are different because they have been apart for so long.

The Caribbean is warm because it is near the middle of the earth (just north of the equator) and gets sun all year round. Warm winds blow across the sea, mostly from the northeast. They are called "tradewinds" because they helped trading ships sail to the Caribbean from Europe.

Sometimes very bad weather and super strong winds blow across the Caribbean toward the United States. These big storms are called hurricanes. They can cause much damage on land and on the reefs.

THE NATURE OF THE OCEAN

When astronauts look at Earth from space, they see a planet mostly covered by water. Some people call our Earth "Planet Ocean." That's because it has much more ocean than dry land.

From space, the world's ocean looks the same all over. But it can be very different from place to place. The water can be different. The location and shape of the holes filled by seawater can be special.

How is seawater different from one place to another? Here are three important ways that seawater can change, depending on:
1. how warm or cold it is
2. how much salt it holds
3. how clear or murky it is

Seawater in the Caribbean Sea flows in complicated patterns called currents. Some currents are warmer and saltier than others. Some currents are on the surface. Some are deep down below.

Oceanographers are scientists who study the ocean. Oceanographers can tell a lot about the currents in the Caribbean Sea by using satellites. Cameras and instruments on satellites record the temperature, movement, and level of the ocean currents on the sea's surface. Oceanographers also use ships to take water temperatures and measure ocean saltiness below the surface.

All this information helps them to do many things—study currents, predict weather, help fishermen find fish, help sea captains save fuel, and a lot more.

≈≈≈≈≈≈≈≈≈≈≈≈≈≈≈≈≈≈≈≈≈≈≈≈≈≈≈≈≈≈≈≈≈

DISCOVER
FOR YOURSELF

Benjamin Franklin and the Gulf Stream

Two centuries ago, Benjamin Franklin studied the very strong currents of the Gulf Stream by using floating bottles and information from sailors. Franklin was interested in the Gulf Stream because he was in charge of the mail. Sailing ships carried important mail to England and France. A sailing ship that found the Gulf Stream could ride it for a fast trip to England.

≈≈≈≈≈≈≈≈≈≈≈≈≈≈≈≈≈≈≈≈≈≈≈≈≈≈≈≈≈≈≈≈≈

MORE THAN SEVEN SEAS—THE MANY WATERS OF THE WORLD

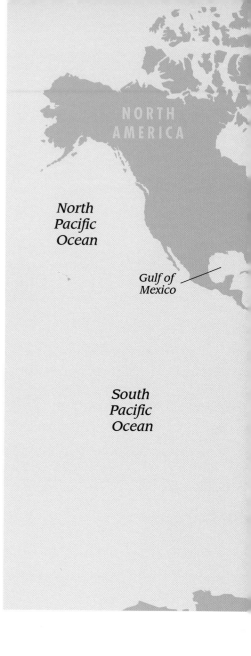

North Pacific Ocean

Gulf of Mexico

South Pacific Ocean

The location and shape of a basin filled by seawater gives each body of water special characteristics. The earth's seawater fits into holes of many different sizes and shapes. These giant holes are shaped by the land around them. The names for these different areas of seawater depend on their size and shape.

An *ocean* is the biggest area of seawater. An *ocean* is so big, it touches several continents. It can take many days to cross an ocean, even in a fast boat. The Pacific Ocean is the world's largest ocean. The Atlantic Ocean and the Indian Ocean are very large, too.

A *sea* is smaller than an ocean but still very big. A sea is more enclosed by land than an ocean and may touch only a few countries or even be in the middle of a single country. Sailing the "Seven Seas" is an old sailor's term. In reality, there are many more seas than seven. The Mediterranean Sea is a big, famous sea. It is connected to the Red Sea by the Suez Canal. The Caribbean Sea touches Florida and Mexico and has many islands.

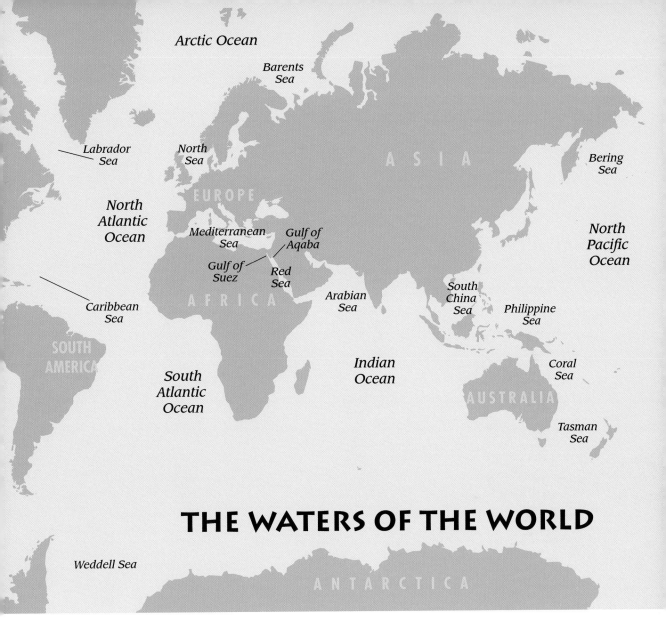

Arctic Ocean

Barents
Sea

Labrador
Sea

North
Sea

A S I A

Bering
Sea

North
Atlantic
Ocean

EUROPE

North
Pacific
Ocean

Mediterranean
Sea

Gulf of
Aqaba

Gulf of
Suez

Red
Sea

AFRICA

Caribbean
Sea

Arabian
Sea

South
China
Sea

Philippine
Sea

SOUTH
AMERICA

Indian
Ocean

Coral
Sea

South
Atlantic
Ocean

AUSTRALIA

Tasman
Sea

THE WATERS OF THE WORLD

Weddell Sea

ANTARCTICA

Smaller parts of the ocean can be called a *gulf*. Sometimes gulfs are big, sometimes small. The Gulf of Mexico is very big. The Gulf of Aqaba (AH-ka-ba) and the Gulf of Suez are small. These gulfs are at the very top of the Red Sea.

WHERE ARE THE INDIES?—
CARIBBEAN LANDS AND ISLANDS

The Caribbean Sea is separated from the Pacific Ocean by the land of North and South America. On the other side, there is a long string of islands called the West Indies. This island chain separates the Caribbean Sea from the Atlantic Ocean. Some of the islands are big, such as Cuba, Haiti, and Puerto Rico. Some are small, such as the Bahamas, St. Thomas, Montserrat, and Grenada.

There are many different kinds of islands in the West Indies. Some are small and made of coral. Some are large and made by volcanoes. Some are made from the sea bottom that has been pushed up by earthquakes. Some Caribbean islands have very high mountains. Others are barely higher than the level of the sea.

DISCOVER FOR YOURSELF

Columbus's Mistake

The great arc of islands in the Caribbean is called the "West Indies." Why is it called the "Indies"? Because Christopher Columbus made a mistake. The real Indies, the East Indies, are far away, near India. They are islands in the Indian Ocean and the Western Pacific Ocean. But, when Columbus sailed into the Bahama Islands in the Caribbean Sea in 1492, he thought he was on the edge of the Indies, so he called it that. That's also why he called the native people he met there "Indians."

The waters of the Caribbean are filled with hundreds of tiny islands.

Almost all Caribbean islands have coral reefs around them. Corals—and all the plants and animals that live on the reefs—thrive in the warm waters. A big coral reef that forms near a coastline is called a "barrier reef." The Great Barrier Reef in Australia is the largest in the world. But the second largest is the barrier reef off the country of Belize, in the Caribbean.

Below left: The barrier reef in Belize is the second-largest in the world.
Below right: A diver swims along a steep coral wall.

FLYING DOWN THE WALLS
OF THE CARIBBEAN

Imagine you can fly just by kicking your legs and moving your arms. Imagine gliding over a sunny field of rocks at the edge of Arizona's Grand Canyon. At the edge, the wall drops straight down, to the sunlit canyon bottom 1,000 feet (305 meters) below.

Of course, you can't fly just by moving your arms—unless you are scuba diving. Water supports a diver much better than air. A diver can glide, dive, climb, and hover. Caribbean reefs are famous for walls as steep as the Grand Canyon. A diver can swim over a shallow sunlit reef. Then he can come to a steep drop that falls 1,000 feet (305 meters) down.

A diver looking down a steep Caribbean reef wall can only see about 200 feet (61 meters). Seawater scatters and stops light. At 1,000 feet (305 meters) down, it would be darker than a moonlit night, even if the sun were shining brightly at the surface. And seawater changes light with increasing depth, too. The red and yellow parts of light are gone by about 40 feet (12 meters) deep. Green and blue light lasts the deepest. That's why red blood from a speared fish looks green to a diver.

◀ **Rope sponges reach out from a steep coral wall.**

A diver needs a bright light to see all the colors of the reef in water deeper than about 20 feet (6 meters). Divers use a powerful flash called a strobe to take colorful underwater photos like the ones in this book.

◀ **Underwater photographers need special equipment and bright flashes to capture images from deep below the sea.**

SEA FANS

Before there were air-conditioners and electric fans, people used hand fans to stay cool. Often fans were beautifully colored and decorated. Many were delicate works of art.

There are beautiful, colorful fans underwater in the Caribbean, too. Tiny, delicate animals build them. But many sea fans are big. Some sea fans are bigger than the chalk-boards in a classroom. Some are taller than an adult human.

Sea fans are relatives of reef corals. Corals build hard, rock-like skeletons. But sea fans build soft, flexible fan-like skeletons. They are often called "soft corals." Many animals live on sea fans as "guests." These guests sometimes feed on the sea fan's polyps. Polyps are the tiny round animals that build the sea fan skeleton.

Tiny animals called polyps create the intricate and beautiful structures of sea fans.

SPONGES BIGGER THAN THE KITCHEN SINK

What color is the "sponge" in your kitchen sink? Pink, blue, brown? But is it really a sponge?

Sponges are simple animals, but they build complex shapes in many colors. Some are shaped like vases, some like barrels, some like ropes or wires. Other sponges form a flat crust on reef rocks.

There are many kinds of sponges on the reefs of the Caribbean Sea. Some are tiny. Others are bigger than a bathtub! Some barrel-shaped sponges are big enough for a diver to hide in. Many have bright colors—red and yellow and purple. Others are dull blue, gray, or brown. Often, tiny animals—crabs, brittle stars, fish—live on or inside sponges. Some sponges use poisonous chemicals as a defense. The well-named "touch me not" sponge causes a painful sting if you do touch it. (But touch it not!)

For many years, divers in the Caribbean harvested sponges to dry and sell. These real sponges dried into light brown lumpy shapes. But not long ago, people discovered a way to make sponge-like stuff from plastic. Now, almost all kitchen sponges are plastic. Real sponges stay on the sea bottom.

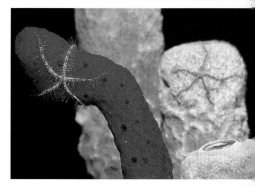

◀ *Top:* **A giant barrel sponge, big enough for a diver to hide inside.** *Middle:* **A brittle sea star sits atop a vase sponge.** *Bottom:* **Sponges grow in a wide variety of bright colors and shapes.**

A SEA OF PLANTS

Most plants on land—grasses, shrubs, bushes, trees—have roots and flowers. But plants in the ocean are different. Seaweeds and kelps have no roots and no flowers. When they attach to the sea bottom they grow special threads to hold on with, but these are not roots.

Some seaweeds float around in the ocean. These floaters grow little bubble-like floats to help them stay on the surface where there is a lot of sunlight. Plants use sunlight to make their food. Fish can't make their own food so some of them eat plants.

Some other kinds of seaweeds make hard crusts on the surface of rocks. These stony crusts are usually red. Although they are plants, they look a lot like coral skeletons.

Left: **Hard, calcified algae covers the bottom of a reef.**
Right: **These tiny clumps of algae grow in the sand and look like tiny "underwater palms."**

There are a very few kinds of plants in the sea that do have roots and flowers. They are called sea grasses. Many parts of the shallow sandy areas in the Caribbean are rich with large beds of sea grass. They look like underwater hay fields. Many animals depend on the sea grass beds. Young fish, shrimp, and snails hide there for protection. Sea horses also live there. In some places, people call sea grass "turtle grass" because of the sea turtles that feed on it.

This kind of algae, called sargassum weed, spends the first part of its life anchored to the sea floor. Later, it floats.

← A hermit crab emerges from the protection of an empty conch shell.

CONCHES—QUEENS OF
THE CARIBBEAN SEA

Imagine a snail with black and yellow eyes and a pink shell bigger than your head. Does that sound like a sci-fi movie? Snails that size are real and they live in shallow sandy places in the Caribbean Sea. People call them "queen conches" (CONKS). Young conches live in the shelter of sea grass beds where they are safe from hungry fish. When conches get bigger, they move out onto the sand where they eat plant matter.

But even big conches are not really safe here. The meat of queen conches has long been a delicious treat for humans. Many Caribbean fishermen take conches to the fish markets. Cooks use conch meat to make chowder and fritters. People have fished for conches for many thousands of years. Jewelry and spoons made from conch shells have been found in ancient Mayan graves. Because so many fishermen take conches, these pink snails are becoming scarce. Some Caribbean countries now have laws to protect conches from overfishing.

A queen conch's eyes are on the end of long stalks.

◀ *Top left:* **Moray eel**
Bottom left: **Cowfish**

◀ *Top right:* **Red grouper**
Bottom right: **Parrotfish**

FISH TEETH—STABBERS, SLICERS, SCRAPERS, AND CRUNCHERS

You can probably tell a lot about what a fish eats by looking at its teeth. Fish that eat other fish often have long, sharp teeth in both jaws. A moray eel uses its long teeth to stab small fish and hold them tightly. Most reef sharks have long, sharp teeth in their upper jaw for stabbing.

Some fish eat plants. Parrotfish have big teeth like the bill of a parrot. They use their beaks to scrape plants from rocks. Triggerfish have stout rounded teeth and strong jaws. They crunch the tips of coral branches and eat the small coral animals.

When they scrape and crunch, parrotfish and triggerfish also swallow pieces of rock and coral. They have special grinding teeth in their throats. These flat teeth grind the rock into sand. Much of the sand on coral reefs comes from the wastes of triggerfish and parrotfish.

A PREGNANT MALE?

Some fish look like fish. Others don't. A seahorse is a fish but it doesn't look like one. (It's also much smaller than a horse!) A full-grown seahorse is about as long as your hand. Its head looks like a tiny horse's head. The snout is long (like a horse's) and shaped like a tube. The seahorse uses its tubular mouth to suck up little animals to eat. The "mane" and "ears" of the seahorse are fins. Just behind the "ears" are the gill slits. Seahorses hang on to seaweed with a wrapped tail—like a monkey uses its tail. The body of a seahorse is covered by hard scales welded together to form an armor.

Father seahorses are very special. They have a pouch to hold eggs and little baby seahorses. The mother seahorse puts her eggs into the father's pouch. When the eggs are fully developed, baby seahorses are "born" from their father's body. He then has the baby-sitting job until the little seahorses can swim and get their own food. Baby seahorses are tiny—about the size of your fingernail.

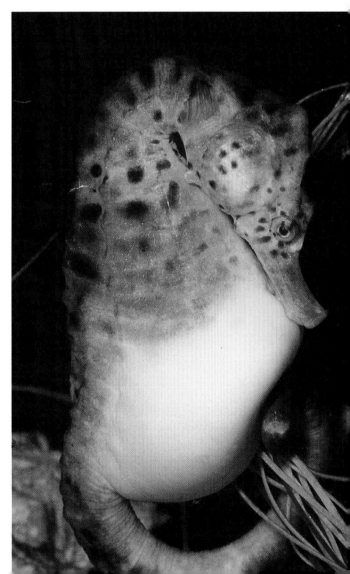

Male seahorses hold fertilized eggs in their pouches until the young are fully developed.

SEA TURTLES

At least three kinds of sea turtles live in the Caribbean. Green sea turtles eat seaweeds and sea grass. Leatherbacks and hawksbills eat jellyfish and sponges.

All sea turtles nest on sandy beaches. A mother sea turtle digs a big hole in the sand. She backs over the side of the hole to lay her eggs. The eggs look and feel like soft ping-pong balls. One mother turtle may lay 100 eggs. When she is through laying eggs, the mother turtle uses her strong front arms to push sand into the hole and bury the eggs. After a month or so, each ping-pong ball egg hatches out a baby turtle about as big as your hand.

Turtle eggs and adults have long been a delicacy for people. Because of the great demand, sea turtles and their eggs have been over-fished, which has threatened the health of the species. In many parts of the world they are now protected and farmed.

A large, old loggerhead crushes mollusk shells as it feeds. *Inset:* **Green sea turtles like this one are protected by international laws.**

HOORAY FOR DOLPHINS!

People love dolphins. Maybe because, of all animals in the sea, they are the most like us. Dolphins are mammals and so are humans. Mammals breathe air. Mammal mothers feed their babies with milk. Like humans, dolphins take care of their young for a long time. Dolphins have very highly developed brains and even seem to smile at us.

The warm, sandy bottomed waters of the Caribbean are great places to see dolphins. The two most common kinds are spotted spinner dolphins and bottlenose porpoises. Another name for the spotted spinner dolphin is the "hooray" dolphin. They make you so happy when they jump and spin, that you want to say "hooray!" Bottlenose porpoises are really dolphins. Sometimes people call dolphins "porpoises." But true porpoises belong to a different family. True porpoises don't have long beaks like dolphins.

All dolphins hunt. Usually they hunt schooling fish, such as herring and sardines. Dolphins also hunt squid and other swimming animals, such as shrimp.

In clear water, dolphins can see schools of fish. But in deep or murky water, how can dolphins find their food? They use high-pitched sounds that are too high for human ears to hear. A dolphin can send out a high-frequency sound and listen for its echo. If the sound hits a fish, the echo will be different than if it hits a rock. Dolphin brains can translate sound echoes. This special skill is called "echolocation." It enables dolphins to use sounds to "see" fish, the terrain of the ocean bottom, and each other.

Opposite: **Two bottlenose dolphins leap from the waters near Honduras.**
Top right: **A bottlenose dolphin chases a school of small fish.**
Bottom right: **A family of Atlantic spotted dolphins.**

"STINGRAY CITY"

It's a good idea to be careful around stingrays. To protect itself, a stingray has a long, thin, sharp spine on top of its tail just behind its round flat body. Often, stingrays lay flat on the sandy bottom. If a careless wader or swimmer steps on a stingray and scares it, the stingray can slash or stab the person's foot.

But in the Caribbean's Cayman Islands, people and a big gray kind of stingray, called the Southern stingray, have learned to have fun together.

Southern stingrays are as big as coffee tables and have strong sharp spines at the base of their tails. Sometimes they rest on the bottom. But they also swim around flapping their fins as if they were wings. In the clear, warm waters over sandbars at a place now known as "Stingray City" dozens of people come by boat to swim, snorkel, wade, and dive with playful stingrays.

Several years ago, fishermen found that stingrays would come to eat the scraps of bait and fish they threw overboard. Now, people come from all over the world to swim and play with the stingrays. On weekdays tourists come. On weekends, families and school kids ride out in local boats to swim and play with the rays.

Giant, 5-foot (1.5-meter) stingrays are plentiful at "Stingray City" in the Cayman Islands. *Opposite:* A diver swims playfully with a huge stingray that has come up to him for food.

SWIMMING WITH THE SHARKS

Large sharks live in the Caribbean Sea. The biggest ones are tiger sharks. They can be as long as a taxicab. Sandbar sharks, hammerheads, bonnetheads, reef sharks, blacktips, silky sharks, nurse sharks, and lemon sharks live there, too.

Until recently, people studied sharks by killing them and cutting them up. Now we can study sharks while they are alive and swimming around. Marine biologists study the lives of lemon sharks in the sandy areas of islands in the Caribbean Sea. These scientists

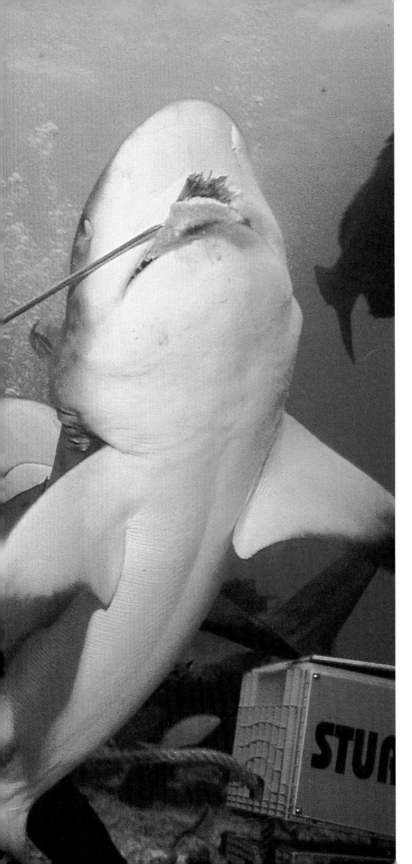

attach tags to the sharks, and the tags transmit sounds. By using underwater microphones, the scientists can hear the sharks and follow them around. Lemon shark pups are only about as long as your arm but full-grown sharks are bigger than your mom and dad.

Using small hooks, scientists catch lemon shark pups. They weigh them, measure them, tag them, and let them go. After a few months, they find them and catch them again. Sometimes they make them vomit so they can see what the pups have been eating. This way, scientists can study the same group of sharks year after year without harming the sharks.

A Caribbean reef shark is fed by a diver.
Inset: **A marine researcher shows how a silky shark becomes immobile when turned upside down.**

GARDENS OF EELS

When divers think of eels on coral reefs, they usually think of moray eels. Morays are bigger than your arm and have sharp teeth. Morays eat fish, crabs, and shrimp. Sometimes they bite divers by mistake when divers stick their hands in the hole where a moray is hiding.

But there are other much smaller eels, too. They live in the sandy areas near the reef. Some animals live buried in the sand; some swim over the sand. Garden eels live half in and half out. They shelter by burrowing holes in the sand and keeping their tails hidden. When scared by a big fish or a diver, a garden eel quickly pulls its entire body and head into the hole. Garden eels move so fast they seem to disappear.

◄ Garden eels poke their heads out
from their sandy hideaways.
Inset: Morays are some of the
Caribbean's largest eels.

TINY "INVISIBLE" BEAUTIES

Observation is the skill of looking very closely and trying to make sense out of what you see. It is probably the most important skill that scientists use. When people first go snorkeling or diving on a Caribbean reef, they are thrilled with the bright colors and interesting shapes. They usually watch the big things—fish, rays, lobsters.

After a few dives, however, most divers learn something important. If you stay still, in one spot, and look very carefully, you can see some wonderful animals that you completely missed on your first dive. Often, these special animals are very small. Usually, they live on or inside bigger animals, such as sponges, coral, and sea fans. Many have adapted wonderful ways of camouflaging, or hiding, themselves. Finding and observing them makes you realize how camouflage allows many creatures to survive. It also reminds you that there is so much life in the ocean that we cannot easily see.

Left: **A cleaner shrimp finds shelter within an anemone.**
Inset above left: **A decorator crab covers itself with tiny sponges as camouflage.**
Right: **The trumpetfish nearly disappears within a cluster of sea fans.**
Below: **The flat peacock flounder lies motionless on the bottom, waiting for unsuspecting prey to swim by. This flounder can also change color to make itself blend with its surroundings.**

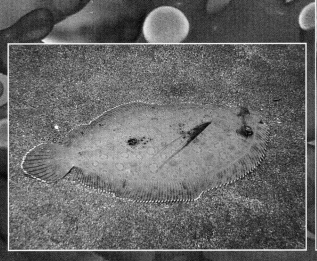

Some Caribbean Sea creatures are easy enough to see—but when you see them, you need to look twice! These animals have features or markings that can "trick" the observer. The porcupinefish normally looks like a spiny swimmer. But, if you scare or threaten it, the small body puffs up to many times its normal size. A fish called a "sea robin" usually looks like a fish, but when it's frightened, it unfolds large, bright wings that confuse and threaten enemies and make it look more like a bird than a fish!

Top: **A porcupinefish**
Middle: **Think you see the large eyes of these butterfly fish? Look again! These "false" eyes make predators think the fish are much bigger than they are.**
Bottom: **The sea robin fans out large wings to confuse its enemies.**

CARIBBEAN SINGERS

Humpback whales only visit the Caribbean during the winter. In the spring, they travel northward along the east coast of the United States. Then they spend their summers in the food-filled waters of Canada, where they feast on fish and shrimp.

During the fall, as the weather turns cold, the humpback whales swim south to warm Caribbean waters. Baby whales, called calves, are born in the Caribbean. Because they are mammals, their mothers feed them with milk.

Humpbacks are the Caribbean's biggest singers. Scientists aren't actually sure why male humpbacks sing. Perhaps their songs tell other male whales to stay away. Maybe the males sing to find a mate. Some whales sing for hours. The sound travels long distances underwater. The songs change from year to year but some themes stay the same.

A huge humpback whale moves gracefully through the ocean water.

CORALS OF FIRE;
SPONGES OF PAIN

Sometimes it is better to look and not touch. Divers and snorkelers in the Caribbean need to be very careful about touching things underwater.

One good reason to be careful about touching is to avoid pain. Some corals and sponges have strong poison cells. They use them to catch food and to keep bigger animals away. When a person touches the coral or sponge, the poison cells can sting and burn. Some hurt only a little bit. Others hurt a lot.

Fire coral is some of the Caribbean's most dangerous coral.
Inset: **Bristleworms can be hard to see, but they sting fiercely.**

Some of the ocean's strongest poison cells are housed in the "fire coral." Fire coral forms coral heads with large whitish-yellow flattened branches. These are common on most Caribbean reefs. The little animals that grow this beautiful structure can burn a diver's skin and cause a painful rash.

Below top: **The touch-me-not sponge stings on contact.**
Below bottom: **The tips of this giant anemone's tentacles contain powerful stinging cells.**

RE-THINKING SHARKS

Not long ago, people thought sharks were all bad. Fishermen were hired to kill sharks and throw their dead bodies away. Sometimes they sold them for their meat and shark skin. Many people—particularly in Asian cultures—like to make soup from shark fins. With demand high, fishermen began to catch a lot of sharks all over the world.

Ideas about sharks have changed a lot in the last 20 years. Now, we are curious about them and need to help them survive over-fishing. Scientists today know a lot more about sharks. Films, photos, and scientific studies have taught us that sharks are not mean, they are interesting. They have also shown us that sharks all over the world play an important role in the life of the oceans.

Left: **A Caribbean reef shark swims above a coral bed.**
Below: **A female blacktip shark.**

HUMANS, HISTORY, AND THE CARIBBEAN

TEMPLES IN THE JUNGLE

The lands washed by the Caribbean are home to many cultures, some ancient and gone. One of the more interesting and advanced cultures was founded by ancient people called the Maya. The Mayan civilization flourished for about 650 years, from A.D. 250 to 900. The jungles (even close to the seashore) of Belize and Mexico hold ruins of elegant Mayan statues and buildings that were made from limestone formed beneath the sea millions of years ago.

An ancient Mayan carving in Belize.

WHO DISCOVERED WHOM?

The Italian explorer Christopher Columbus (who explored for Spain) thought he had "discovered" the "West Indies." But people with well-developed cultures had already been living there for centuries. Some tribes were called Arawaks. Others were called Caribs. The name "Caribbean" comes from the name of the Carib people.

Then Columbus and his men showed up. They must have looked pretty strange to the Caribs and Arawaks. Did Columbus discover them, or did they discover Columbus?

THIEVES AND HEROES

The Caribbean Sea has a long history of sailing adventure. Columbus visited the Caribbean four times. Later, during the 16th to 18th centuries, the sea was a special place for thieving sailors called pirates. Pirates used their ships and cannons to steal merchant cargo.

The governments of some countries hired pirates to rob the ships of enemy countries. These pirates were called "privateers" or "buccaneers" and they were considered heroes. In the 16th century, Spanish ships filled with treasure sailed across the Caribbean. England was an enemy of Spain, so the English government hired pirates to rob the Spanish. The privateers were allowed to keep the treasure in return for sinking the Spanish ships.

The Caribbean has always been a risky place for sailing because of its shallow coral reefs. Many pirate ships were wrecked on Caribbean reefs. Today, divers look hard to find the wrecks of old pirate ships. The soft sandy beaches made good places to bury things—especially treasure. Some people think the wrecks and the island shores still contain secret fortunes buried by the ruthless pirates of the Caribbean.

This engraving depicts the famous pirate Captain Kidd burying his treasure on a Caribbean island.

SWIMMING WITH DOLPHINS

Swimming with dolphins in a swimming pool or sheltered lagoon is a popular tourist activity in the Caribbean. There has always been a strong bond between humans and dolphins. Some people say dolphins even try to communicate with humans. Other people, including some scientists, are afraid that too much tourist interaction may not be good for either dolphins or humans.

Humans have learned a lot from dolphins. Wild dolphins and dolphins in oceanariums have shown us how echolocation works. By studying the behavior and language of dolphins, humans are also learning a great deal about animal intelligence and how animal language is organized. Observing the complex social system of dolphins has also taught us much about how animals live together and cooperate in the wild.

Snorkelers play with a bottlenose dolphin in a Honduran lagoon. *Opposite:* **Researchers are studying the effects of human interaction on wild dolphins.** *Opposite inset:* **Dolphins learn fast and are easy to train.**

HOW DO YOU MAP AN OCEAN?

A taxi driver can find an address by using a map and street signs. But how can a sailor find a location on the broad, empty ocean? When a boat sails near land, sailors can recognize landmarks. A map, or even a drawing of mountains and cliffs and beaches, can help them find their way. Some of the first maps made by sailors were made on the Red Sea. We know that the Egyptian Queen Hatshepsut sailed the length of the Red Sea about 2,500 years ago.

But in the open sea, away from land, there aren't any signs. And how can you make a map of a place that is all ocean?

Here's how: All mapmakers have agreed on two kinds of imaginary lines that cover the earth. One set of lines go from the top of the earth—at the North Pole—to the bottom of the earth—at the South Pole. These are the lines of "longitude" (lonj-EH-tood). The other lines go around the earth from east to west. These are the lines of "latitude" (lat-EH-tood). The latitude line that goes around the fattest part of the earth (at its middle) is the called the equator. Above the equator is the Northern half of the earth, also known as the Northern Hemisphere. Below the equator is the Southern part of the earth. That's the Southern Hemisphere.

The equator is easy to find on a globe. But mapmakers also divide the earth in half going north to south. This line divides the world into two halves, too—the western half and the eastern half. Every line is numbered with degrees as they move around the circular earth.

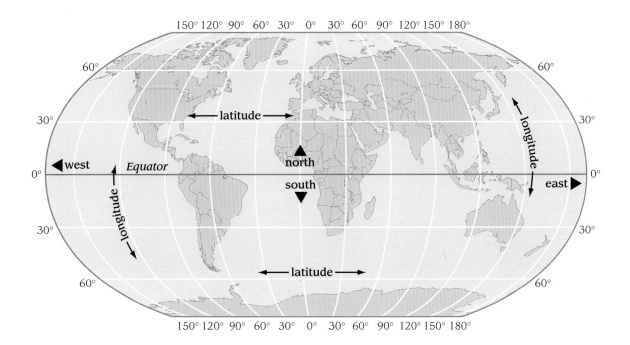

You can find the Caribbean Sea on a map of the world by using "positions." A position is the place where a particular place on the latitude and a particular place on the longitude meet.

Find the longitude line for 75 degrees west. Find the latitude line for 15 degrees north. The two lines will cross in the Caribbean Sea.

But such lines only appear on maps. Nobody can actually draw them on the ocean! So how do sailors find their positions? By looking at the sky! At any given time, the moon, stars, and the sun are in predictable places. If a navigator knows what time it is and can measure the location of the sun, moon, or a few stars, he or she can find a position on Earth.

A new and easier way has recently been invented. Navigators can use small computers that use satellites instead of stars to find a position of latitude and longitude.

GLOSSARY

Equator The imaginary line of latitude that goes around the waist of the Earth (from east to west).

Gulf Stream A very large warm current that flows from the Caribbean north along the east coast of the United States.

latitude Imaginary lines that go around the earth from east to west (side to side). Map makers draw them on maps to show where places are located.

longitude Imaginary lines that go around the earth from north to south (up to down). Map makers draw them on maps to show where places are located.

navigation Finding where you are (your **position**) by using mathematics, time, stars, and maps.

position The exact place where someone or something is, described as a point where a specific latitude and specific longitude meet.

salinity the amount of chemicals dissolved in seawater. The salinity of pure water is zero; the salinity of seawater is more than 3%.

FURTHER READING

Clarke, Penny. *Beneath the Oceans* (Worldwise series). Danbury, CT: Franklin Watts, Inc., 1997.

Greenberg, Keith. *Marine Biologist* (Risky Business series). Woodbridge, CT: Blackbirch Press, 1996.

Morgan, Nina. *The Caribbean and the Gulf of Mexico* (Seas and Oceans series). Chatham, NJ: Raintree/Steck-Vaughn, 1997.

Savage, Stephen. *Animals of the Oceans* (Animals by Habitat series). Chatham, NJ: Raintree/Steck-Vaughn, 1997.

INDEX

Caribbean Sea
  countries bordering, 4–5, 12
Colors
  of fish. *See* Fish
  of oceans, 3, 15
Columbus, Christopher, 12, 42
Coral and coral reefs, 7, 13–16, 22, 33–35, 38–39
Crustaceans, 7, 17, 19, 33

Divers, 14–15, 17, 28, 33–35, 38–39
Dolphins, 26–27, 44

Eels, 22, 33

Fish
  babies, 23–24, 25–26, 30–31, 37
camouflage, 35
colors of, 3, 16–18, 20–21, 28, 34
eggs, 23 25
eyes, 20
fins, 23, 28, 41
gills, 23
mouths, 23
poison, 17, 38–39
sounds, 27, 31, 37
tails, 23, 28
teeth, 22, 33
Franklin, Benjamin, 9

Gulf Stream, 9
Gulfs, 4, 11

Islands, 5, 10, 12–13, 28

Mapping, 46–47

Mayan civilization, 21, 42

Oceans, 6–8, 10, 12

Panama Canal, 6
Pirates, 43
Plants, 18–19, 22

Sea or saltwater, 8–10, 15
Sea turtles, 19, 24–25
Seas, 10–11
Sharks, 22, 30–31, 41
Snails, 19–21
Sponges, 7, 17, 35, 38
Stingrays, 28
Suez Canal, 10

Weather, 7, 9, 37
West Indies, 12, 42
Whales, 37